Hal•Leonard
INSTRUMENTAL
PLAY-ALONG

TENOR SAX

Christmas SONGS

T0068331

CONTENTS

To access audio visit:
www.halleonard.com/mylibrary

3071-0847-3593-4664

Audio Arrangements by Peter Deneff

ISBN 978-1-4950-2555-6

HAL•LEONARD®
CORPORATION
7777 W. BLUEMOUND RD. P.O. BOX 13819 MILWAUKEE, WI 53213

Visit Hal Leonard Online at
www.halleonard.com

ALL I WANT FOR CHRISTMAS IS YOU

TENOR SAX

Words and Music by MARIAH CAREY
and WALTER AFANASIEFF

THE CHRISTMAS WALTZ

TENOR SAX

Words by SAMMY CAHN
Music by JULE STYNE

HAPPY HOLIDAY

from the Motion Picture Irving Berlin's HOLIDAY INN

TENOR SAX

Words and Music by
IRVING BERLIN

I WONDER AS I WANDER

TENOR SAX

By JOHN JACOB NILES

I'LL BE HOME FOR CHRISTMAS

TENOR SAX

Words and Music by KIM GANNON
and WALTER KENT

LET IT SNOW! LET IT SNOW! LET IT SNOW!

TENOR SAX

Words by SAMMY CAHN
Music by JULE STYNE

MARY, DID YOU KNOW?

TENOR SAX

Words and Music by MARK LOWRY
and BUDDY GREENE

THE MOST WONDERFUL TIME OF THE YEAR

TENOR SAX

Words and Music by EDDIE POLA
and GEORGE WYLE

MY FAVORITE THINGS

from THE SOUND OF MUSIC

TENOR SAX

Lyrics by OSCAR HAMMERSTEIN II
Music by RICHARD RODGERS

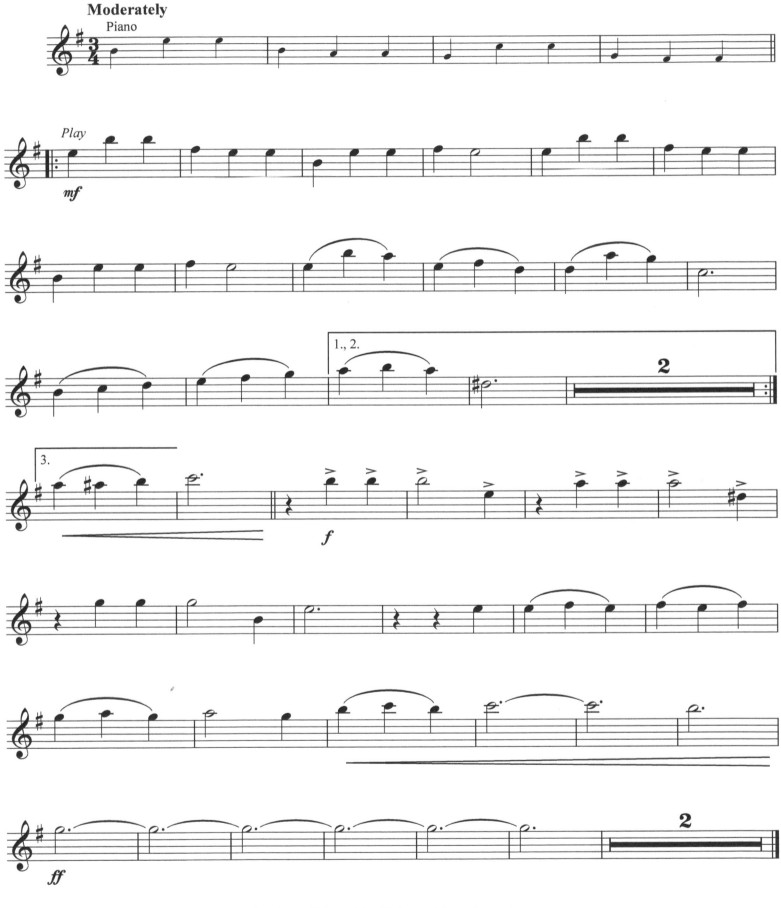

SILVER BELLS
from the Paramount Picture THE LEMON DROP KID

TENOR SAX

Words and Music by JAY LIVINGSTON
and RAY EVANS

THIS CHRISTMAS

TENOR SAX

Words and Music by DONNY HATHAWAY
and NADINE McKINNOR

WHITE CHRISTMAS
from the Motion Picture Irving Berlin's HOLIDAY INN

TENOR SAX

Words and Music by
IRVING BERLIN